HOW TO WRITE
Dinosaur
JOKES

WITH BESTSELLING AUTHOR

DAVID
BEDFORD

SOME JOKES

What did Dinosaurs have that no other
animal has now?

Baby Dinos! Awwww!

What is huge, green and smelly?

A Brachiosaur's big toe!

What do you call a Velociraptor with a
Pterodactyl on his head?

Silly!

How do you know which little Dinosaur
lives in your fridge?

By the footprints in the butter!

How do you give a Spinosaurus a
goodnight kiss?

Wait until he's asleep!

Do you know how long Dinosaurs
lived for?

Just the same as SHORT Dinosaurs!

What's heavier than a Seismosaurus?

TWO Seismosauruses!

What would you call a Dinosaur that moves like a Kangaroo?

TriceraHOPS!

How can you tell if you have a Gigantoraptor in your bed?

She has a large G on her pyjamas!

How many Dinosaurs fit inside your lunchbox?

I don't know, you'd better open it and see!

A Herbivore eats plants. A Carnivore eats meat. But what kind of Dinosaur eats EVERYTHING?

An Omnomnomnomnomnovore!

What did the young Dino want in his
bedroom at night?

Meteorlights!

Where do Dinosaurs like to hang out in
the park?

On the see-saw-osaur!

What came AFTER the Dinosaurs?

Their tails!

Which Dinosaur comes to your house for
a sleepover and then goes home again?

A Stay-Go-saurus!

What Dinosaur has eight wheels?

A Vulcanodon on two skateboards!

Where do Dinosaurs go for holidays?

To the Dino-SHORE!

And where do they buy their beach sandals?

At the Dino-STORE!

Then what do they shout when they've finished their ice-creams?

'Dino wants MORE!'

What makes more noise than one hundred T-Rexes?

Two hundred T-Rexes!

What's as big as a Dinosaur, the same shape as a Dinosaur, and moves just like a Dinosaur — but weighs nothing at all?

A Dinosaur's SHADOW!

Why to Pterodactyls have wings?

So they can dino-SOAR!

Why were the meat-eaters shy of the new dinosaur?

Because they'd never seen herbivore!

Who were the Jurassic superheroes?

TriceraCOPS!

How did Dinosaurs build a treehouse?

With Stegosaws!

What do you shout when an Allosaurus
takes a penalty?

DINO SCORES!

What did the twin Dinosaurs with wobbly
teeth say?

'It's-so-sore-us!'

What do you call a Spinosaurus with
headphones on?

Anything you like, it won't hear you!

What do you get when a Diplodocus
sneezes?

Sticky!

What do you call an armoured Dinosaur
who plays out in the rain?

StegosauRUSTY!

What did the heavy, armoured Dinosaur
say after he fell over?

'My ANKLE-is-sore-us!'

When do Dinosaurs sit down to eat cake?

At TEA-Rex Time!

What's faster than a Velociraptor on a
bike?

TWO Velociraptors in a Ferrari!

Which Dinosaur breaks your toys?

Tyrannosaurus Wrecks!

What do Dinosaurs use to make their
bedroom floors warm, soft and colourful?

Carpet rep-tiles!

Who's the scariest Dinosaur?

A TERROR-dactyl!

Why wasn't the Megalosaurus allowed to
go swimming?

Because he didn't say pleeeeziosaur!

**And what is the VERY BEST and
most BONE-TINGLINGLY FUNNY
Dinosaur Joke EVER told?**

Wait for it ...
Are you ready?
Okay, here it is:

Nobody knows — it's gone extinct!

Or
is
it
one
YOU
know?

See if you can write down some Dinosaur Jokes you know already.

Then, when you're finished joking, we'll have a look at all the ways to write even more really, really good Dinosaur Jokes. Read on!

WRITE YOUR DINOSAUR JOKES HERE!

JOKES, WHAT ARE THEY?

J okes can be *anything* we say that makes us laugh, smile — or groan!

What's a Dino's favourite number?

Eight!

They can be funny stories, or any made-up sentences that make us giggle. They can even be poems.

> *A Tyrannosaurus called Trevor*
> *Read books and learned how to*
>   *be clever.*
> *Everyone knew his name*
> *When he quickly became*
> *The first T-Rex in Outer Space*
>   *Ever!*

You can easily make up your *own* jokes, and your own jokes will be the funniest of all. Here's one I made up that really makes me chuckle,

Which Dinosaur has TEN eyes?

An Iiiiiiiiicthyosaur!

Jokes can be about all kind of things, of course. So why am I making this book full of *dinosaur* jokes?

I'll tell you why ...

DINOSAUR JOKES

D inosaurs are funny!
Why?
I don't know!

Why was the giant lizard so funny?

Because it ... was?

Is it their friendly, funny *shapes*?
Or are dinosaurs funny because of their *bones*?
Or because they're so *big*?!

**What's BIGGER than an
Argentinosaurus?**

*I don't know, but it has just eaten my
sandwich, and now it's looking at yours!*

Would giant-sized DOGS be funny? Or cute but enormous KITTENS?

All I know for sure is this: every time I start to write a story about dinosaurs, I know I'm going to be smiling all the way through. I've even written a whole book of funny poems about dinosaurs. Here's one,

A Dinosaur with a big braino
Never plays on a smoking
*   volcano.*
If they're asked to go play
They just chuckle and say,
'Play on a volcano? No way no!'

Just after I'd finished writing that *Limerick* poem, I thought up my first *ever* Dinosaur Joke:

Why did Diplodocus NEVER have a bath?

Because he didn't want to be ex-stinked!

Ha ha?

I'm sure lots of people have made up that joke before.

Of *course* they have.

But I'd never heard it. To me, my joke was like

a bright, shiny, glittery, twinkly bit of treasure I'd discovered all by myself. Wheeee!

So, could I write LOTS of jokes, and make them all about those funny dinosaurs?

Why ever not?!

Why did the Human make up lots of Dinosaur jokes?

Because he wanted to TRYceratops!

In this little book, I'll share with you how I wrote my Dinosaur Jokes. And I hope you'll join in and write your own ones, too.

Let's start right away ...

FINDING OUT

If you want to write your own Dinosaur Jokes, you need to get dinosaurs *on the brain*! Don't worry, it doesn't hurt ...

Why did the Apatosaur, Dilophosaurus, Gallimimus and Utahraptor go to the doctor?

They were feeling JurasSICK!

Having dinosaurs on your brain just means thinking about dinosaurs ... finding out about dinosaurs ... and remembering what you know already about those big-boned riotous reptilians.

Which Dinosaur knows ALL the clever words?

The Thesaurus!

Here are some words about dinosaurs and the Dinosaur World that will help us get started. You can come back to this Chapter anytime you want to get in the mood to make up more jokes.

Dinosaur Words

Lizards, armour, aquatic, lagoon, swamp (a smelly swamp).
Ice-age, Triassic, Jurassic, Pleistocene (sounds like plasticine …).
Meteor, extinction, fossils, bones, skeletons, vertebrae, palaeontologist
(a scientist, knows a lot).
Ankylosaur, Brachiosaur, Hadrosaur, Pterosaur, Ichthyosaur, Stegosaur — and all the other *osauruses*.
Triceratops, Sauropod, Diplodocus.
Plates, sail-backs, spines, horns, heads, long necks, big bodies, jaws and teeth!
And long tails.
Herbivores eat plants.
Carnivores eat meat. Omnivores eat anything!

Which Dinosaur doesn't know ANY of these clever words?

The Not-a-Thesaurus!

Can you think of more things you know about dinosaurs and their world? If you do, then write them down.

Draw some pictures too, if you like.

Think dinosaur, dinosaur, DINOSAUR!

Write down as many dinosaur *names* as you can. I mean, their *scientific* names, like *Tyrannosaurus* and *Spinosaurus* and *Dilophosaurus* and so on.

Not their *real* names, like Barry and Ma Lee and Kevin and Ulrika ... (I made those up).

When you're ready, let's get on with writing our first type of joke ...

WRITE YOUR DINOSAUR FACTS HERE

5

DINOSAUR NAME JOKES

To make our first kind of joke, we're going to play with dinosaur names. Their *scientific* names, of course!

Let's choose *Triceratops*.

I like the way that sounds,

Tri - cer - ra - tops

Splitting up the word like that makes me think of something funny right away:

Tri - cer - ra - bottoms!

That's *very* silly ... and I love it. So let's try making a quick silly joke. How about,

How did the Triceratops go down the slide?

On his tricerabottom!

Ha, ha, ha and he, he, hee!

There will be lots more jokes ending with the same last word, bottoms ... but I'll leave those up to you. (Where do Triceratops babies wear their nappies or diapers? How does a Triceratops sit on a chair? We could go on being silly forever!)

Let's try another dinosaur name,

Stegosaurus

Splitting the word should help us,

Steg - oh - saw - us

I'm getting a joke right way, and I'm sure you are as well. Here's mine,

Why couldn't we give the Dinosaurs a huge surprise party?

Because Stego saw us!

But hang on! LOTS of dinosaur names end with saurus/**saw us** ... so the answer could be,

Because Apato saw us
Because Tyranno saw us
and even,
Because the Dino saw us!

This idea of 'saw us' made me look through my book about Dinosaurs, and see if any other names could help me make a longer joke.

Here's what I was able to write,

Why did our Dinosaur surprise party go wrong?

Because ...
Stego saw us
Apato saw us
Tyranno saw us
Brachio saw us
and then ...
Pakicetus tried to eat us!
(And he didn't even say pleaseiosaur!)

Now it's over to you.

Try splitting up some dinosaur names and see if you can find a joke inside them.

You can work things out in your head (quite hard!), or by writing down (easier).

To start you off, here are some dinosaur names I've split up.

Supersaurus
Soop - er - saw - us

Archaeopteryx
Ar - key - op - ter - rix

Pteradactyl
Te - ra - dac - til

Piatnitzskysaurus
Pee - at - nit - ski - saw - us

(I can see a few giggles in that one!)

It might be fun to use some *rhymes*, too. So I think we should do some rhyming next ... read on!

WRITE YOUR DINOSAUR NAME JOKES HERE!

6

DINOSAUR RHYMES

Rhyming is really helpful for making lots of memorable jokes. Let's jump straight in by seeing what rhymes with *Dinosaur* ...

Rhymes with Dinosaur

store, shore, snore, paw, claw, door, floor, roar, raw

Do you know any *more*? Are you really *sure*?!

I'm already getting some joke ideas. How about,

Who's the best at waking everyone up at night?

A SuperSNOREous!

Or you could say,

Why can't you sleep at night in the Jurassic?

Because of the Dino-SNORES!

Snoring is funny. I can imagine some colourful pictures of snoring dinosaurs, or one great, big SuperSNOREous keeping the other dinosaurs from going to sleep.

Any more rhymes giving you ideas? Of course, we could rhyme *Dinosaurs*,

What do you call a Dinosaur who delivers presents at Christmas?

Santa Claws!

or it could be,

What do you call a T-Rex who delivers presents at Christmas?

Santa JAWS!

There must be other ways of writing this joke. How many can you think of?

TOP WRITING TIP: As an author, I'm always thinking of different ways of writing the same thing. I try out the different ways, and choose which I like best. It's what authors do, for hours and hours!

Thinking up rhymes is an easy way to make up Dinosaur Jokes, so have a go yourself.

Take your time.

And when you're finished, we'll look at another, very strange kind of joke ...

WRITE YOUR RHYMING JOKES HERE

REALLY ODD JOKES!

I've always liked really *odd* jokes. I mean really, *really* odd jokes. So odd, they're not even jokes. They're just ... strange.

Why did the Albertosaurus cross the road?

Because it was Tuesday!

Why did the Utahraptor put eggs in its ears?

I don't know, I can't hear you!

I mean, they're not even funny, are they? But they're … something.

Really Odd Jokes are almost too easy to write, so why not have a go and see if they work for you too?

The trick is to let your mind wander away, far away, from what might normally come next.

What do you call a Stegosaurus with a Tyrannosaurus Rex on her head?

Orange!

What's yellow and green and orange and red?

Dinosaur Secrets!

Very, very odd! Now to something *hilarious* …

WRITE YOUR REALLY ODD JOKES HERE

KNOCK KNOCKS

'Knock Knock!'
'Who's there?'
'Annie Dinosaur!'
'Annie Dinosaur who?'
'Annie Dinosaur you like! RAA!'

Even when we were young and hardly bigger than Allosaurus eggs, if someone said,

'Knock Knock!'
we soon learned to reply,
'Who's there?'

And then we'd wait for something funny to be said, so we could laugh until our breath ran out.

At least, that's what *I* probably did!

Here is a Knock Knock I hear often, from a 5-year-old,

5-year-old Joker: **'Knock Knock!!!!!!!!'**
Most of the class: 'Who's there?'
5-year-old Joker: **'A *banana* ha ha ha ha!'**
(rolls about laughing)

Now that's really only *half* a joke, but it works — especially if you're 5 years old.

Here's our 5-year-old's *Dinosaur* Knock Knock (I'm sure you know what's coming ...)

'Knock Knock!!!'
'Who's there?!'
'A *Banana DINOSAUR* ha ha ha ha ha ha ha ha ha ha ha ha!'
(rolls about laughing even more)

Just like a Brachiosaurus with a mammoth-sized bag of swamp-flavour corn chips, Knock Knock jokes are rarely alone ...

If someone tells a Knock Knock, someone else will usually want to tell their own favourite one, as well.

'Knock Knock!'
'Who's there?'
'Olive!'
'Olive who?'
'Olive with Dinosaurs!'

And then nothing can be done until *everyone* has told their Knock Knock.

'Knock Knock!'
'Who's there?'
'Dinosaur!'
'Dinosaur who?'
'No, *Owls* go 'Hoo'. Dinosaurs go ROOOOAAAAARRGGH!!!'

In school, the class teacher usually has a good one ready to go.

'Knock Knock!'
'Who's there?'
'Interrupting T-Rex!'
'Interrupting T-Re - '
'RAAAAAAAAAGGH!!!'

All this roaring is scary, huh?!

There is a different kind of Knock Knock that goes on for longer. Here's one I knew when I was a kid, only I've made it about dinosaurs now, of course,

'Knock Knock!'
'Who's there?'
'Uncle Archaeopteryx.'

'Knock Knock!'
'Who's there?'
'Uncle Allosaur.'

'Knock Knock!'
'Who's there?'
'Uncle Spinosaurus.'

'Knock Knock!'
'Who's there?'
'Uncle Ankylosaurus.'

'Knock Knock!'
'Who's there?'
'Auntie.'
'Auntie who?'
'Auntie you glad all those uncles have gone away?!'
(groan!)

Here are a few more Knock Knocks I've made up.

'Knock Knock!'
'Who's there?'
'Supersaurus Boo!'
'Supersaurus Boo who?'
'Boo hoo? Don't cry, he won't eat you!'

'Knock Knock!'
'Who's there?'
'Icecream T-Rex!'
'Icecream T-Rex who?'
'I scream T-Rex when I see T-Rex coming!!!'

'Knock Knock!'
'Who's there?'
'Ammonia!'
'Ammonia who?'
'Ammonia little dinosaur, so let me in!'

'Knock Knock!'

'Who's there?'

'Stegosaur Wah!'

'Stegosaur Wah Who?'

'Wahoo? You DO like Stegosaurs a lot, don't you?!'

I'm sure you already know LOTS of Knock Knocks yourself, so why not change them to be about dinosaurs?

Try them out on a friend, and see how they work.

Now let's try a completely different kind of joke ...

WRITE YOUR KNOCK KNOCK JOKES HERE

9

WOULD YOU RATHER?

People *always* like being asked what they think about things.

Would You Rather **... your teacher was
a Pteradactyl
OR
your dentist was a Tyrannosaurus
Rex?**

That's quite a lot to think about! What would *you* choose? I'd rather my teacher was a Pteradactyl, because she can fly around the classroom above my head and see what good work I'm doing.

(And I would LOVE to get a sticker for writing this page!)

Would you rather ... share your
lunchbox with a Spinosaurus
OR
ride home on the back of a
Velociraptor?

I'd take the Velociraptor home, and hold on tight!

Would you rather ... play football
against THE ANKYLOSAURS
OR
play basketball for THE
SUPERSAURUSES?

Definitely football for me ... but I would try not to get an *ankle oh sore*! (groan)

There's not much more to say about how to write Would You Rathers — it's more fun making them up than talking about them!

Would you rather ... write some Would
You Rathers of your own now
OR
be chased by a roaring
Huehuecanauhtlus into the next
Chapter?!

WRITE WOULD YOU RATHER? JOKES HERE

SILLY SENTENCES

This chapter is all about being silly with words.

In fact, you need to be sillier than you have *ever* been before!

So let the silliness begin!

Dinosaurs were born before sandwiches.

Did you know, Dinosaurs invented the whirl?

Kinds of whirl invented by Dinosaurs are ...

**tractor whirls
whirls on hats
hamster whirls**

Yes, I *am* just making things up! Which reminds me ...

TOP WRITING TIP: now that you've started being silly, keep going! Who knows where it will take you? And if it takes you nowhere or you get stuck, you can just start over. That is what authors do ALL the time. Now back to the silliness ...

Dinosaurs were the first creatures to wake up in the morning.

Until Dinosaurs started it, everyone got out of bed after lunch.

***Flying* Dinosaurs were the first to get cloudy.
FACT: Clouds are made of fuss and wool and some have ice bobs inside their tummies.**

The First Dinosaur came from the
First Dinosaur Egg.
But was it *really* the first though?
Answer: Yes.

When Dinosaurs invented
sandwiches, it was the start of the
Sandwichic Period.

Sandwiches should really be called
Dinosaurses.

The best *Dinosaurses* for Sandwichic
picnics are,
ham and pickle
cheese and pickle
egg and sauceosaurusness

TOP **FIVE** DINOSAUR **FIRSTS**!

First whirl on a hat
First running like you're wobbly like
jelly
First to cut a pizza into triangles
First hiding under a bed
First forgetting where you left your
lollipop

So you can see, Dinosaurs did most things first. And they were able to do so because they were *interested*.

THE END

Have a go at writing your own Silly Sentences. Try not to stop until you reach the end of the page. Then stop!

Next it's time to play the newly invented GAME OF JOKES ...

WRITE YOUR SILLY SENTENCES HERE

GAME OF JOKES

Now let's play a game.

As you know already, lots of jokes are *questions*.

'Why did the Diplodocus *never* have a bath?'

But what if the person you're joking knows the answer already? Or, after thinking for a bit, they work it out for themselves?

'Uh ... is it because it didn't want to be, uh, EX-STINKED or something?'

Then your joke is going to be as dead as a Daspletosaurus.

All you can do is say 'Sorry!' and go hide in the washing basket.

And cry.

Boo hoo hoo.

The best way to *stop* that happening (and especially if you're joking with someone who's a very good guesser/joke-teller/smart guy) is to be ready with *more than one answer!*

This is what I call the **Game of Jokes**.

And to play the game, you have to be *ready to play*.

Here's how it works,

Game of Jokes I

Ace Joker (You!): 'Why did the Diplodocus *never* have a bath?'
Smart Friend: 'Oh, I know this one! It's because he didn't want to be *ex-stinked!*'
Ace Joker (You!): 'NO! It's because baths weren't even *invented* in the Dinosaur times! Didn't you *know* that?!!!'

So YOU win the game!

You could be ready with *lots* of answers, and be able to tell your jokes knowing that you will *always* have the last laugh.

Let's see how it works if you have lots of answers up your sleeve.

Game of Jokes II

Ace Joker (You!): 'So why did the Diplodocus *never* have a bath?'
Smart Friend: 'Is it because he didn't want to be ex-stinked? Or because baths weren't invented?'
Ace Joker (You!): 'NO! Haven't you seen a Diplodocus? If they had a bath, there'd be no room left for the water!'
OR
Ace Joker (You!): 'NO! Because it wasn't a Tuesday!'

Now let's try finding different answers to some more joke questions.

This is the time to get your thinking cap on. (If you've got one.)

'What do you get when a Diplodocus sneezes?'

Hints: If you're unlucky, when that gigantic sneeze happens, you might get wet! Or sticky. Or something even more horrible!

But you might also get something for the Diplodocus, to help him feel better — a tissue, or a hot water bottle, or even his Mum!

Now think up different answers to this question,

'How can you tell if you have a Gigantoraptor in your bed?'

Hints: He might have a large G on his pyjamas of course! But have a think ... if there was a gigantic dinosaur in your bed, how would you notice? Does he cuddle your toys, or read your books? And what might he have done with your pillow, if he was hungry?!

Write down all the answers you think up.

Really, you're writing lots of *different* jokes.

And it's *always* good to have lots of different jokes written down.

You never know when you need a really good joke.

Especially one you made up all by yourself, and that's so good *nobody* will guess the answer.

So, after waiting longer than it takes a baby Diplodocus to find the end of her tail to nibble ...

now
it's
YOUR
turn!

'What do you get when a Diplodocus sneezes?'

Answer 1:

Answer 2:

Answer 3:

Answer 4:

Answer 5:

'How can you tell if you have a Gigantoraptor in your bed?'

Answer 1:

Answer 2:

Answer 3:

Answer 4:

Answer 5:

12

AND NOW IT'S YOUR TURN

In this book, you've read about different kinds of jokes.

Name Jokes and Rhyme Jokes
  Really ODD jokes
  Knock Knocks and Would You Rathers
  some *extremely* Silly Sentences
  and even a few Limerick poems too,

> *An Albertosaurus named*
>   *Freddie*
> *Always had lunch in his beddie*
> *He ate ALL his greens*
> *A whole plate of baked beans*
> *And six mangoes he squashed on*
>   *his headdie!*

But does this book have the greatest dinosaur joke EVER?

Well ... I don't think so. In fact, I really hope not. And that's because I know for sure that *someone* (and I mean *YOU*) can think up a better one!

So please, please, PLEASE, make up a BRAND NEW, brilliant, shiny, rib-tickling, glittering joke that makes you shout 'WHEEEE!'.

A joke that is SO funny, the stiff old dinosaur skeletons standing bored in our museums will all jangle their old bones, and rattle their bony skulls, as they have a secret little giggle about it!

Have fun. Smile. And remember: always be a

Try-try-try-tryceratops!
(groan!)

THE END

PLEASE WRITE A REVIEW!

Authors love hearing from readers!
Please let me know what YOU think about

(How to Write) Dinosaur Jokes

by leaving a review on your favourite online bookstore, or on Goodreads. (Though remember, if you are under age 13, you **must** ask a legally responsible adult to guide you online.)

Were the jokes funny? Has this book helped you be a better writer? And, most importantly of all — did you ENJOY it?!

Writing reviews is another really great way to practice and enjoy writing.

Why not **write a Dinosaur Joke** in your review? I'll be hugely delighted to read it!

Thank you!

David Bedford
www.davidbedford.co.uk

for a first look at David's funny and exciting new fiction series for ages 7 to 13!

'WE HAVE COME TO WIN YOUR PLANET!'

Football Sam v Aliens United

Chapter 1: The Shooting Stars

'Every time The Shooting Stars get on a football pitch,' complained Dexter, *'everything* goes wrong!'

'New teams always have trouble settling down,' said Football Sam. 'Don't they?'

Just one week before, Sam had signed up The Shooting Stars to play in the JFL five-a-side football league. Sam, along with Dexter and their team-mates, had been given free, shiny football kits. And they'd had their picture taken for the JFL website, with The Shooting Stars cheering and waving their arms about madly, as if they'd won their first trophy.

It had been the best day of Football Sam's life.

Now, Sam's team, who were ready to play in their sapphire-blue shirts, shorts and socks, stood about on a field in the middle of nowhere. There wasn't a sign of their opponents, and to make matters even worse, Sam and his friends were surrounded by thick, white fog that completely blotted out the Saturday morning sunshine.

Dexter stretched out his arms in front of him. His lime-green goalkeeper gloves disappeared into the fog, then reappeared when he brought them back to hug his sides.

'This f-f-fog is really *f-f-f-freezing*,' Dexter said, shivering. 'I want to go back to bed!'

'We'll be okay,' Sam promised, watching his breath make a ball-shaped cloud in the icy air. He stamped his boots on the ground. 'We just need to warm up.'

'I'm not so sure about that,' said Mai Lee, The Shooting Stars tall, dark-haired defender.

'What do you mean?' said Roo, bouncing lightly on her strong striker's legs.

'I *mean*,' said Mai Lee, 'that this looks like yet another total and utter disaster! I'm sorry, Sam, but this team isn't working.'

Sam couldn't think of a reply. The Shooting Stars had already played two warm-up games, and neither had gone to plan. On Tuesday, after school, they'd lost heavily to the West Runton Rovers. And on Thursday night, under the floodlights in the park, they'd been beaten again, this time by Unicorns United, whose players were all much younger than Sam and his team-mates. Mai Lee was right. So far, The Shooting Stars wasn't working at all.

'We'll all feel better when we've scored some goals,' Roo said, sounding upbeat.

'There's been *twenty-seven* goals scored *against* us!' Mai Lee reminded her.

Max, The Shooting Stars left-back, pushed out his chin proudly. 'Thirteen of those goals were *penalties*,' he said, delightedly. 'And they were *all* because of *me*!'

Mai Lee turned to her partner in defence, and scowled at him. 'Max,' she said, 'you just *can't* be a defender!'

'Why not?' Max replied, innocently.

'Because,' exclaimed Mai Lee, 'you think giving away penalties is clever!'

Max grinned. 'Yeah,' he said. 'I do. I've made the most penalties in a game, ever.'

Football Sam stared unbelievingly at his team-mate. How could awarding their opponents penalties make Max feel so happy?

'Max, you're *so* annoying!' Mai Lee said, through her gritted teeth.

'I know!' said Max, grinning wider.

'Why can't you play somewhere else, like midfield?' Mai Lee suggested.

'Why don't *you* play somewhere else,' smirked Max. 'Like, on another team?'

'*You*,' said Mai Lee, looming over her team-mate as her anger bloomed, 'ought to play on another *planet*!'

'You can go play in another *galaxy*!' replied Max, chuckling.

Roo barged between Max and Mai Lee, to cool things down.

'Things don't *always* go wrong when we play,' Roo said. 'Don't forget, Dexter *saved* a penalty against the Rovers.'

'The ball hit him on his nose!' snorted Mai Lee.

'Well,' said Roo, stubbornly, 'Football Sam nearly scored against the Unicorns.'

'Sam's free kick hit a seagull!' cackled Max.

'The problem isn't just the games we've lost,' Dexter said, grimly. 'This time, *we* are lost! Where *is* this place?'

The Shooting Stars all turned to Sam, who'd been slowly shaking his head as he watched them argue. A team was supposed to be supportive. Stick together. Help each other out. Sadly, The Shooting Stars players didn't seem to care about their team-mates at all.

In answer to Dexter's question, Football Sam shrugged. 'I don't know where we are,' he admitted.

Sam replayed their morning's journey, hoping that he hadn't somehow made a silly mistake.

They had taken two bus rides, the second dropping them right out in the middle of the countryside, and from there they'd had to follow a map. Their way led down a muddy lane, through a herd of goats, along rows of cabbages, and finally to where they were now. Sam and his team-mates had quickly changed into their football boots, and dropped their sports bags in a pile.

Sam wasn't sure, though, if they were standing on a football pitch at all. The grass was quite long and tufty. Maybe it was just a farmer's field. Sam began thinking uneasily about what farm animal might be lurking, unseen, in the thick fog.

'You never did say who we were playing?' said Roo.

'There wasn't a name,' Sam said. 'I told you – it was just a map.'

An envelope was posted through Sam's door on Monday morning. It had

`Your Saturday Fixture`

written on it, in large purple letters. Inside the envelope, Sam had discovered the map, with instructions about which buses to catch.

'Maybe the other team are already here,' said Roo, 'and are lost in the fog, too?'

'HEY THERE!' Max suddenly bellowed, and his team-mates jumped.

Sam waited, holding his breath. Making noise wasn't a good idea. If there *was* an animal in this field …

Suddenly the fog began to move. It swirled about them, speeding up until it was spinning furiously. Sam huddled with his team-mates, the wind howling in his ears and pulling at his football top and shorts, while a blur of brilliant white whipped past his eyes.

'We're inside a tornado!' Mai Lee hollered urgently.

'This is well weird!' yelled Max, sounding like he was enjoying himself.

But even as Max spoke, the fog began rising

upwards, thinning to pale wisps that were speckled with blue from the bright sky above.

When the fog had completely cleared, Sam, shading his eyes with his hand, could finally see his team-mates clearly.

Roo was looking past him. 'Over there!' she said, pointing. 'It looks like a huge ...'

Sam spun around, but what he saw wasn't anything like he'd expected.

'What *is* that?' said Dexter, nervously.

Chapter 2: Aliens United

A gigantic, grey metal leg, as tall as the towers that hold floodlights above a football stand, stood at the far edge of the field. At its foot, a silver football boot as big as a house was planted firmly on the ground.

Copying his team-mates, Sam squinted upwards, open-mouthed, to see what could be perched on top of a gigantic, grey metal leg.

Max was the first to speak.

'Oh,' he said happily, as if he'd just worked out a puzzle. 'It's a big, round, purple spaceship!'

As if in reply to Max, the sound came for the first time, a loud

Whooomm!

and The Shooting Stars all gasped as the big, round, purple spaceship bathed them in a purple spotlight. There was a smell like bubblegum – Sam could almost taste it. Then, one by one, purple shapes began to form, standing on the grass not far away. The shapes were figures of ... not *people*, exactly ...

'*They're aliens,*' Sam heard Roo whisper. '*Aliens from Outer Space!*'

'*Noooo!*' Dexter whimpered in horror. He tugged on the sleeve of Sam's shirt. 'You know I don't like aliens. Not even in comics!'

Dexter let go of Sam and staggered backwards, his eyes wide as he watched one of the purple alien figures walk towards them.

'It will be all right,' Sam said quickly, trying to stay calm and not panic the rest of his team, who had already retreated several paces.

Sam's gaze flipped back to the alien. It was now standing just an arm's length from him. Sam goggled at it. The alien had a long purple face with one yellow eye in the middle of its forehead, and a flat, round nose like a button. Its mouth was small, red and curved upwards at the edges – it reminded Sam of a jellybean.

Sam glanced nervously to his left and right. Three more purple aliens were watching him. They were taller than the one in front of Sam, but otherwise they looked the same. Their red jellybean mouths curled up at the edges, too.

'I think they're friendly,' he said over his shoulder to his team. He couldn't believe how normal he sounded – inside, he was shaking, and his heart was thumping hard and fast, like the hooves of a running horse.

Turning again to the aliens, Sam realised they were wearing football kit. Their tightly fitting shirts and shorts were exactly the same purple colour as their two arm-like tentacles, and their two short, stocky legs. Their purple football socks ended in purple football boots that had two dazzling white stripes on the side. There were words on the stripes, printed in black capitals. Sam could read them clearly:

`ALIENS UNITED`

Sam heard himself speaking his thoughts aloud. 'They're a football team,' he said, feeling a small smile crease his cheeks. 'They've come here to play!'

As he spoke, the spotlight from the alien spaceship widened until it flooded the entire field, and then began flickering rapidly. Sam closed his eyes. When he opened them again, he saw that the ordinary farmer's field they were standing in had been transformed into a state-of-the-art football pitch. He scanned brand-new goalposts and nets, crisp circular centre and penalty spots, short-cropped grass, and freshly made line markings. His smile widened.

Then he focused on the goal area to his left.

In it, and moving slowly towards the goal-mouth, was a blob-shaped alien as big as a gorilla, and as round and orange as an orange. Sam watched it stretch out at least eight long, feathery tentacles, before coiling them neatly around its body.

Dexter made a noise that sounded like, 'Gaggh!'

Sam uttered a small, easy laugh, and gave The Shooting Stars goalkeeper a thumb's up. 'That's just their goalie, Dex!' he said, soothingly.

The small, purple alien in front of Sam was

holding out a tentacle. Sam, feeling his heart gallop even faster, shook it gently. It felt warm, and sticky like a unwrapped lollipop. Then Sam jerked his hand away in sudden surprise as another loud

Whooomm!

came from the spaceship overhead, and a computer voice spoke:

'GALACTIC FIXTURE NUMBER THREE TRILLION AND ONE! THE SHOOTING STARS PLAY ALIENS UNITED!'

'This is going to be awesome!' he told his team-mates. 'We're playing a team of aliens – how cool is that?!'

The alien wiped its tentacle on its shirt, before speaking in a quick, squeaky voice that reminded Sam of his sister's Guinea Pig, Kevin.

'We have come to take over your planet,' the alien squeaked. 'Okay, good?'

Then, rubbing the end of its tentacles together, it declared,

'Let the winning of Earth begin!'

from
Football Sam v Aliens United

Ebook & Paperback

More info:
www.davidbedford.co.uk

ABOUT THE AUTHOR

David Bedford is the best-selling author of more than 85 books for children.

When he's not making books, or practising and teaching *tai chi*, David visits schools around the world to promote reading, tell stories, coach writing, and share what he knows about being a creative person.

For more info about David (including about when he was a beardy scientist) you can check out his website here:

www.davidbedford.co.uk

Printed in Great Britain
by Amazon

75111902R00047